CONTENTS

ACKNOWLEDGMENTS

I would like to express my gratitude to many people who saw me through
the book; to all those who provided support, talked things over, read,
wrote, offered comments, allowed me to
quote their remarks and assisted in editing, proofreading and design.

Special thanks to Patricia and Festus for their help in researching and
writing the book.

1 POULTRY FEEDS FORMULATION

Poultry Feeds Formulation can be defined as the step by step process of combining feed ingredients in order to form a uniform mixture for chicken in order for them to meet the required nutritional requirements in their diet. When considering formulating feeds formulation, cost should be on your mind. Cost is the most important factor in business especially in the poultry business, therefore it is important to mix the various ingredients in order to achieve all the nutrients required by chicken and save on cost eventually. Another factor you should take into consideration is the digestibility of the feeds. The feeds that you feed on your chicken should be digestible so that the chicken can be have to have the required nutrients at the right time. Lastly you should ensure that the feeds that you formulate should be palatable so that the chicken can be able to feed on them.

2 NUTRITIONAL REQUIREMENTS FOR POULTRY

1. WATER

Water plays an important role in the diet of poultry. Chicken can not live without water because it will stop them from growing and they lead to poor egg production for laying chickens. Water requirements may vary depending on the climatic conditions, protein quantities in the diet and the salt contents in the feeds. Avoid by all means water that has toxic substances as i will be exploring more on these toxic substances. Caution should be exercised on water that are given to your chicken.

2. PROTEINS

Chicken need high protein contents in their diet so as to help in growth rates and good egg production. These feeds are fish meal, bone meal, peanut cake, soya bean meal etc. Chicken use the amino acids found in protein to develop their feathers and skin. Amino acids also helps the chicken in the formation of soft tissues.

3. CARBOHYDRATES

These are starchy elements that are found in grains.

4. MINERALS

The important mineral components in the body of chicken are Calcium, Phosphorus, Magnesium, Sodium and Potassium. Calcium is important for the development of the bones. Calcium also plays an important role in laying birds as it helps in improvement of eggshell, this is the reason as to why some hens lay eggs and they stop laying hens for no apparent reason however much you feed them. It is therefore recommended to ensure that you feed your chicken with diet that contain calcium if the eggshells are few.

5.VITAMINS

Vitamins are an important nutritional requirement in the diet of poultry. Vitamins can be categorized into two. These are;

. Water soluble

. Fat soluble

Water soluble are Vitamin C and Vitamin B complex whereas Fat soluble are Vitamin A, Vitamin K, Vitamin E and Vitamin D. Vitamin A contains carotene which is an essential component required in the development of good quality yolk.

6. FATS

Fats are essential for the chicken to produce the required energy in order to improve feed conversion rates. An example of foods that contain the required fat content is corn.

3 FEEDS AND ALTERNATIVE FEEDS FORMULATION

FEEDS AND ALTERNATIVE FEEDS

Poultry should be fed on feeds. Feeds can be gotten from manufacturers as per age and weight requirements of chicken. These feeds are usually manufactured so that they can be able to meet the required nutritional requirements of chicken. These feeds can be categorized as follows;

1. Starter feeds

2. Grower feeds

3. Breeder feeds

1. Starter feeds

These feeds are normally fed on chicks as soon as they are hatched and fed on for a while. Starter diet should be fed on chicks for one month and two weeks. Starter diet plays an important role in young chicks because it gives them the right nutrition.

Starter diet contains an average of 19% protein content which is important for the chicks to grow quickly and to become healthier.

2. Grower feeds

These feeds are sometimes referred to as developer feeds and they are fed on developing or growing chicks.

3. Breeder feeds.

Grower feeds contains approximately 16% protein content and they play a important role in a healthy growth maintenance. Chicken that lay table eggs should be fed with layers feeds. Layers feeds contains an average of 15% protein content and some calcium which aids in strong shells for egg laying chickens. Layers feeds should be fed on chicken as soon as they start laying eggs. This can be done around 20 weeks of age as soon as the chicken begins to lay eggs.

It is recommended to provide a large feeding space for your chickens so that the chickens can be able to get enough feeds. Good quality feeds helps the chicken to grow faster, good egg quality and they become resistant to various diseases.

POULTRY FEEDS FORMULATION

These feeds are normally fed on chicken that lay eggs. They are sometimes referred to as layers feeds.

Chickens should be fed on a balanced feed rations as soon as they are hatched until they start laying eggs so that you can be able to improve production and profitability.

ALTERNATIVE HOMEMADE FEEDS FOR POULTRY

With increasing costs of feeds for poultry, farmers are now looking for cheaper methods for their chicken so that they can improve production and profitability. Chicken feeds constitutes of up to 75% of the cost of poultry production. With the increasing cost of feeds, many poultry farmers are now exiting the business thus it is advisable to know the various alternative sources of poultry feeds. For you to be successful in poultry business, you need to ensure that you feed your chicken with quality feeds so as to improve the growth rate and good egg production rates.

These feeds are;

1. Maggots meal

Maggots contain a high source of protein which helps in the development of chicken. The flies lays eggs in areas that are infested with dirt. These maggots appears from the egg in warmer areas in a span of 7 to 20 hours. The maggots begin feeding immediately on and they develop in the material that the egg has been laid on. Animal manure is the most proffered nutrient substrate so as to be able to provide a great substrate for development. It is recommended to use little manure so that larvae can develop easily. A mature maggot can crawl up to 55 feet to a dry, cooler place near breeding stage and lead to pupae stage. A maggot meal contains an average of 48 protein content, 26% fat and 8% fiber content. Maggot meal also contains 17 amino acids which are Lysine, Methionine etc. , calcium and vitamins which helps the chicken maintain good body condition. Since maggot meal contains high protein content and protein being the number one important mineral content in the body of chicken, it then compensates the lacking protein content from commercial feeds. Maggots helps the chicken to become healthy and to produce large eggs for laying chickens. Maggots can be produced for sale or for feeding on chickens.

Maggots have a short lifecycle and they should be fed on the chicken within 10 days of harvesting before they can develop into adults.

. The flies lay eggs in the substrates

. Maggots feed for four to five days before they ca move to pupae in a dry area.

. Adult flies then feeds on decaying organic matter, it does this by liquefying the food using saliva by regurgitating droplets.

. The flies then mate and lay eggs during the period of feeding. In order to get large populations of flies, it is recommended to get them from small amounts of the substrate.

A step by step method

. The materials to be used for maggots production are plastic containers which are normally within our reach, a basin etc. The size should be enough to accommodate the number of maggots you want to breed and the container should also be open.

. The substrates used for maggots production are garbage heaps or manure. The substrates by products to be used are maize shaft, rice bran, wheat offal and cotton bran.

. Mix some amount of water with sugar, molasses, wheat bran or chicken droppings. Chicken droppings should be stored in water for 1 or 2 days. then allow the mixture to stay for 24 hours, covering it in a cool and dry place. The water mixture should then be mixed with the substrate of your choice until it forms a mesh and it does not waterlog the substrate. The plastic containing the substrate should then be left open in an isolated place with no interference. The flies will be automatically be attracted to the sweet mixture. The flies will have increased by 3 days. after 5 days you will notice a large number of white dots in the mixture. Immediately you notice that, which is usually between day 5 and day 6, close the open part of the plastic container with a mosquito net so that you minimize anything from entering the container. The plastic should be kept in a dry place that is cool with some shade so that they are prevented from direct sunlight. The maggots will start hatching from day 6. Bakers yeast can be sprinkled on them to act as a booster for growth so as to increase weight and size, but they can as well be left to grow naturally.

. Harvesting can be done after the 7th day to the 12th day with regards to the chicken you want to feed them on.

2. Mealworms

Mealworms are larvae of the darkling beetle. These mealworms are normally found in grain stores, household items etc. A female beetle lays around 600 eggs over a short period of time. The eggs then hatch within weeks to produce larvae.

Mealworms contains a lot of proteins which help the chicken lay alot of eggs. Mealworms helps cut down the cost of production and improve profitability. Mealworms are becoming important to most farmers because of their efficiency in reducing kitchen waste to compost. This compost is referred to as Vermicomposting or Worm castings are a great source of fertilizer for planting crops. Vermicomposting has a great source of humic acids which helps the condition of the soil and contains important nutritional requirements for the soil like Phosphorus, Nitrogen and Potassium and for that reason keeping mealworms will benefit you in all ways.

Mealworms contains a high protein content. Chicken should be fed on mealworms at the growing stage, laying stage and when the chicken are sick.

Step by step on how to keep Mealworms;

. Materials needed are;

Container

Food scraps

Bedding. Bedding to be used can be compost manure, fallen leaves or any organic material that has been composted.

. Clean and dry the container to be used. It is recommended to use large plastic bins that has lid for the container. A transparent container is required for easy monitoring.

. Drill some holes at the bottom of the container to be used for drainage and the top for ventilation. The size should be chosen based on the waste that you will use.

. Worms and food scraps should then be added. The food scraps to be added can be wheat bran, chicken mash, or cereal crumps. It is recommended to buy Red wigglers Eisenia Fetida from online store because they are best for composting or you may get them from the local nurseries.

. Feed them and watch them grow. For better results, they should be fed regularly.

. It takes few months to hatch to larvae, collect them then feed them to your chickens. The pupa should be kept so as to be used for producing more mealworms.

3. Fodder

Fodder can be fed on chicken to act as an alternative source of feeds. The grains that can be used to make fodder are as follows;

. Oats

. Wheat

. Barley

. Rye

The choice of the above grains is because of their easiness in digestibility. Fodder however should not be fed on chicken with large quantities.

The materials required for growing fodder are;

. Water

. Bucket

Step by step process on how to grow fodder

. Put your grains in a bucket then soak them overnight

.Get containers like plant trays or a basin then drill small holes beneath it to allow water to drain. the holes should be small enough so that the grains do not escape.

. You should then add your grains to the basin then add water.

. The grains should be moist until they start sprouting. The fodder should be set up in a sunny place to allow them to grow at a faster rate. The fodder should be watered on a daily basis.

. The fodder will begin to sprout after 4 to 7 days.

. Flip the fodder upside down once it reaches a desired length then cut from the bottom from the roots. You should then feed your chickens the ready fodder.

4. Homemade Chicken feeds

The ingredients normally used for chicken feeds formulation are as follows;

Millet

Millet is considered an important meal in the diet of poultry as it contains a lot of fats, vitamins and minerals. Millet also contains Phosphorus and Magnesium. Millet provides a lot of amino acids and they help the chicken during the process of digestion.

Sunflower seeds

Sunflower seeds are good for chicken as they contain protein content which is important in the body of chicken. Sunflower seeds also helps the chicken in prevention of E.coli, Brochitis and Coccidiosis in chicken.

Kelp

Kelp also referred to as Seaweed contains 30% nutritional value of grains. Kelp contains Calcium, Minerals, Sodium , Calcium and Magnesium. Kelp can be added to a ratio of 6 to 14% of the diet.

Flax seed

Feeding chicken on flax seed causes increase in Omega-3 fatty acids egg content.

Wheat

Wheat contains a lot of proteins and carbs. Wheat also contains a lot of proteins and amino acids as compared to corn that is why it is recommended to use wheat over corn. Wheat improves digestibility in chickens and they are good in prevention of Coccidiosis.

Oats

Oats have a high protein and fiber content.

Peas

Peas contains protein and amino acids which plays a important role in the diet of chickens.

Making chicken feeds at home

Making chicken feeds at home for your chicken is important as it helps in reducing the cost of production and increasing productivity. Chickens require amino acids and Digestible Crude Protein (DCP) in all their feeds in order to have a balanced feed ration. Good quality feeds improves growth in chickens and good egg production. Amino acids play an important role in the diet of chickens as they help up their growth. Adding feed additives like minerals, vitamins and micro nutrients is important so that the chicken can have balanced feeds that meet the nutritional requirements. The ingredients that you choose to make feeds with should have high protein content and nutritional requirements for chicken.

Layers feed

Chickens can be fed on electrolyte and Vitamin supplements. This can be done for one week. Green crops and lettuce can then be added on regular basis to the diet.

POULTRY FEEDS FORMULATION

Procedure for making 100 kgs layers feed

Ingredients required;

. 18 kgs of soya

. 12 kgs of maize bran

. 47 kgs of whole maize meal

. 6 kgs of limestone powder

Step by step process;

1. Add maize bran, fish meal, soya, whole maize meal and limestone powder in a container then mix all the ingredients together until they are fully combined.

2. use a stick to stir the ingredients until all the ingredients are fully dispersed through out the container.

3. After mixing, the chicken can either be fed on a feeder or you can as well put them in a clean place for the chicken to eat. The feeds should be stored properly so that none goes to waste.

Young layers should be given a diet that has a protein content of an average of 17 percent. This is important to the diet of young chickens so as to help them grow faster and make them get prepared for the stage of laying eggs.

Procedure for making broilers feed

Ingredients required;

. 10 kgs of alfafa meal

. 10 kgs of rolled oats

. 5 kgs of calcium powder

. 7 kgs of poultry nutrients balancer

. 66 kgs of ground roasted soya beans

. 107 kgs of cracked corn

. 10 kgs of fish meal

Step by step process

1. Add cracked corn and ground roasted soybeans in a container then mix the ingredients until they are fully mixed.

2. The mixture should then be stirred with a stick until they are fully mixed. Then stir the rolled oats, fish meal and alfafa meal into the mixture. If incase you do not have fish meal you can as well use bone meal. The mixture should then be stirred properly until they are fully dispersed.

3 The nutrient balancer for poultry and aragonite should be added to the container.

4. The ingredients should then be mixed thoroughly so that the powders are distributed very well in the feeds.

5. The feeds should then be fed on the chickens. This can be done by placing them in the feeder or placing them in the ground that is clean. Once you feed them on your chickens you should ensure that you store the remaining feeds in a place that is dry and cool place for up to three months. Feeds to be fed on chicken should be free from molds and mice.

5. Kitchen scraps

You should feed your chicken on food scraps like fruits. Fruits contain a wide range of minerals, vitamins and antioxidants which are important in the diet of chicken. Examples of these fruits are bananas, water melons, berries and figs. You may want to feed them on grains too, these grains are wheat, rice or corn. Lastly, you should feed your chicken on Vegetables that are fresh, examples of these vegetables are broccoli, carrots, cabbage, kale etc.

6. Restaurant left overs

Restaurant left overs are foods that did not make it to the customer table or foods that the customer left after eating. The process of recycling leftovers can be a great way to reduce production costs in poultry farming and improve profitability. It is of great importance to understand which leftovers are good for your chicken and which ones are harmful. For you to be successful in poultry business, you should look for various ways of cutting costs. You can strike a deal with any restaurant around you so that all the leftovers can be kept for you instead of them disposing them. Feeding your chickens with food waste is a great opportunity for you to provide a balanced feed ration for your chicken.

These are the food scraps you can feed your chicken on;

Vegetables and Fruits waste

Chickens love the taste of all cooked vegetables and fruits waste nutritious. However you should exercise caution on some foods like raw or greenish potatoes, eggplants and avocado pits.

Grains and bread

Chicken love the taste of bread. Chicken should be fed on bread scraps but great observation should be taken so that you do not give them bread that have mold. Mold contains toxic contents and this can harm your chicken, so if you notice any mold in bread scraps you should dispose them. Bread scraps contains nutritional requirements required for proper maintenance of poultry health.

Fish and meat

Chicken love the taste of cooked meat and fish. As with fish, it is recommended to feed them on lobster shells, the skin of fish and shrimp shells. Exercise caution on fish bones because the bones can choke the chicken. Although chicken love the taste of meat, you should never feed them on chicken meat as they can easily be infected with various diseases.

Eggshells

Eggshell is an important nutritional requirement for poultry. Eggshell scraps should never be allowed to go to waste. Eggshells contain Calcium, an important nutritional component responsible for development of strong bones and the development of eggshells that are of high quality.

7. Forage

Forage feeds are alternative sources of feeds available to poultry keepers because of their readiness in availability and because they are cheap as compared to other poultry feeds which are expensive. The utilization of forage materials is important for the chicken to enable it to grow well and to produce quality and healthy eggs. Forage feeds for poultry is not only important to the diet of chicken but also it is important to the nutritional requirements of humans, that is why feeding forage on poultry is a blessing in disguise to humans. It is therefore recommended to plant crops and grasses that add nutritive value to the body of chicken in order to improve on quality standards. Chicken should be fed or allowed to feed on forages. Forages contain nutritional requirements like Vitamin E. It should be noted however that chicken should not feed on too much forages because forages contain fiber which is an indigestible carbohydrate, this means that the digestive system may find it hard to digest. Chicken can be fed on dietary fiber like rice bran, alfafa and wheat middling which improves the availability of nutrients.

8. Sunflower seeds

Sunflower seed is a by product of oil extraction and is best for chicken due to its high level of protein content. Sunflower seeds should be included in the diets of broiler chicken at an average of 16% to 18% in their diet. Sunflower seeds have a sweet taste that is why chicken love them.

9. Mashed potatoes

Mashed potatoes can be used as alternative source of chicken feeds however caution should always be taken so that they are not given green potatoes. Green potatoes produce solanine which is toxic which is harmful to chicken and people. It is therefore recommended to use white potatoes to make mashed potatoes. Sweet potatoes are considered best as they do not produce solanine and they have a sweet taste to chicken.

10. Peanut meal

Peanut meal is a by product that is generated from the extraction of oil. Peanut meal is also referred to as groundnut meal. Peanut meal helps in improvement of broiler meat. Peanut meal also helps improve the yolk quality of eggs.

11. Corn and cobs

Corn is an alternative source of poultry feeds. Corn is the most preferred alternative feed for poultry because of its low fiber content and easiness in digestibility. Corn has the following nutritional requirements;

.An average of 8% protein content

. 1600 kcal/lb energy content for poultry.

. 85% Dry matter content

. 0.18% Methionine content

. 0.24 Lysine content

. 0.07 Tryptophan content

. 0.29% Threonine content

. 3.5% crude fat content

. 0.01 Calcium content

. 0.28 Phosphorus content

. 11% Ash content

Corn should be fed on poultry or should be mixed with other feeds because it improves the quality of the egg.

12. Pasture

Pasture acts as an alternative nutritional requirements for poultry. Pastures should be readily available for poultry throughout the year therefore it is recommended to make plans for the next season. Poultry should be fed or allowed to feed on pasture but not in large quantities because pasture is needed in small quantities to only add up to the overall nutritional requirements of poultry.

13. Herbs

The herbs that chicken can be fed on are;

. Calendula

Calendula herb has a lot of Omega 3 and lots of Vitamins which plays an important role in the diet of chicken. Calendula also has anti-inflammatory component which helps the digestive tract of chicken.

Calendula should be mixed with chicken feeds on daily basis for better results.

. Oregano

Oregano herb is good for the chicken because it helps the respiratory system and it also contains anti bacteria which is good for the chicken.

Oregano should be mixed with chicken feed on daily basis for better results.

. Thyme

Thyme is also called Thymus Vulgaris. Thyme contains omega- 3 which helps the chicken maintain a good healthy condition. Thyme also anti bacteria which helps the chicken combat many diseases. Thyme is rich in iron, Vitamin A and Vitamin B6, Calcium and Manganese. Thyme can be added to chicken feed on fodder

4 FOODS NOT TO FEED ON POULTRY

1. Raw potato peels

Raw potatoes contain alkaloid solanine which contains a very bad toxic substance. Therefore caution should be exercised when feeding your chickens that it should not contain raw potatoes or potato peels.

2. Onions and garlic

Onions and garlic contain an unpleasant taste and this taste will be felt in the taste of the eggs, therefore it is recommended not to feed them on onions and garlic.

3. Avocado skins and pits

Avocado skins and pits contains a fungicidal toxic called Persin which is risky to your chicken because of its poisonous nature.

4. Caffeine and rotten foods

The caffeine in coffee is not good for your chicken, therefore it is recommended to avoid it. Rotten foods on the other hand is not good for your chickens because rotten foods produce toxin which is poisonous to your chicken. Caution should be exercised when feeding your chicken so that you do not harm your chickens.

5. Greasy foods and chocolate

Greasy foods are not good for your chicken because of their hardness in the process of digestion therefore it is recommended to avoid them at all costs. Chocolate also contains toxic substance called theobromine which is poisonous. Chocolate should never be fed on your chickens.

6. Processed foods

Processed foods should never be fed on chicken. An example of processed food is Pizza

ABOUT THE AUTHOR

Davies Cheruiyot is an agribusiness specialist with a degree in agribusiness. He turned to Farming in 2015 considering the untapped potential in the industry. He is the author of Cattle Feeds Formulation, A Beginners guide to Pig Farming, A beginners guide to ginger farming and several other farming books.

Made in United States
Troutdale, OR
05/30/2024

20224497R00022